NOV - - 2021

THE WORLD ALMANAC

AWESOME TRUE-or-FALSE QUESTIONS FOR SMART KIDS

THE WORLD ALMANAC

AWESOME TRUE-OR-FALSE QUESTIONS FOR SMART KIDS

WORLD ALMANAC BOOKS

World Almanac books may be purchased in bulk at special discounts for sales promotion, corporate gifts, fund-raising, or educational purposes. Special editions can also be created to specifications. For details, contact the Special Sales Department, Skyhorse Publishing, 307 West 36th Street, 11th Floor, New York, NY 10018 or info@skyhorsepublishing.com.

Published by World Almanac, an imprint of Skyhorse Publishing, Inc. 307 West 36th Street, 11th Floor, New York, NY 10018.

The World Almanac™ and The World Almanac and Book of Facts™ are trademarks of Skyhorse Publishing, Inc. All rights reserved.

www.skyhorsepublishing.com

10 9 8 7 6 5 4 3 2 1

Cover design by Kai Texel
Illustrations by Alex Paterson

Page composition/typography by Joshua Barnaby

Library of Congress Cataloging-in-Publication Data is available on file.

Print ISBN: 978-1-5107-6745-4
Ebook ISBN: 978-1-5107-6746-1

Printed in the United States of America

THE WORLD ALMANAC AWESOME TRUE-OR-FALSE QUESTIONS FOR SMART KIDS

USER'S NOTE

On the front side of every page, you will find true-or-false statements. Some answers might be easy and others will not! Give each one your best guess, or use them to challenge a friend.

Then turn the page. You will find the correct answers right there, on the back side of each page.

The next page will have even more fun true-or-false tidbits to keep you guessing until the very end!

THE WORLD ALMANAC

AWESOME TRUE-OR-FALSE QUESTIONS FOR SMART KIDS

Food

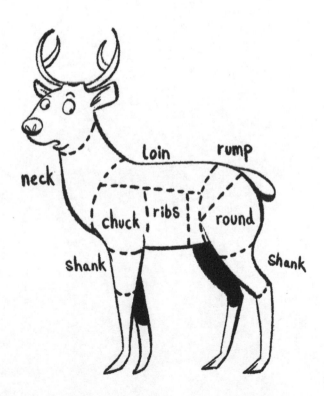

1. Peanuts are not nuts.

   TRUE OR FALSE? → → → →

2. Almonds are closely related to peaches.

   TRUE OR FALSE? ➤ ➤ ➤ ➤

3. Ancient Romans ate spaghetti and tomato sauce.

   TRUE OR FALSE? ➜ ➜ ➜ ➜

4. Tomatoes are a fruit.

   TRUE OR FALSE? ⇒ ⇒ ⇒ ⇒

See the back of the page to find out.

1. **True.** Peanuts grow underground and are legumes, not nuts.

2. **True.** Almonds grow on trees and the part that is eaten is considered a seed, not a nut.

3. **False.** Tomatoes didn't arrive in Italy from the Americas until the 15th or 16th century.

4. **True.** Because tomatoes form a flower and contain seeds, they are considered a fruit.

5. POTATOES ORIGINATED IN IRELAND.

    TRUE OR FALSE? ⇨ ⇨ ⇨ ⇨

6. MOST ORANGES HAVE 14 SEGMENTS.

    TRUE OR FALSE? ⇛ ⇛ ⇛ ⇛

7. McDONALD'S WAS THE FIRST AMERICAN FAST FOOD RESTAURANT TO OPEN LOCATIONS IN CHINA.

    TRUE OR FALSE? → → → →

8. BROCCOLI, CABBAGE, CAULIFLOWER, AND KALE ARE ALL THE SAME SPECIES OF PLANT.

    TRUE OR FALSE? ✏ ✏ ✏ ✏

9. KETCHUP WAS ONCE SOLD AS A MEDICINE FOR STOMACH ISSUES.

    TRUE OR FALSE? ➤ ➤ ➤ ➤

See the back of the page to find out.

⇨ 5.   **False.** Potatoes were not introduced to Ireland until the late 16th century. They originated in South America.

➠ 6.   **False.** Most oranges have 10 segments, which are called carpels.

➔ 7.   **False.** KFC was the first American fast food restaurant in China.

🖉 8.   **True.** All of these cruciferous vegetables belong to the same plant species.

➥ 9.   **True.** In the 1830s, ketchup was sold to people as a cure for indigestion.

10. Deer meat is called "walleye."

TRUE OR FALSE?  → → → →

11. Caesar salads were invented in Ancient Rome, home to emperors who had the title of Caesar.

TRUE OR FALSE? ➡ ➡ ➡ ➡

12. Corn tortillas have been a staple food for thousands of years.

TRUE OR FALSE? ⇨ ⇨ ⇨ ⇨

Answers for previous page.

→ 10. **False.** Deer meat is called venison. Walleye is a fish.

➡ 11. **False.** Caesar salad is believed to have originated in Mexico in 1924.

⇨ 12. **True.** There is evidence of tortillas dating back to 10,000 BCE.

13. FRESH POTATOES CAN BE BLACK.

TRUE OR FALSE? ⊃ ⊃ ⊃ ⊃

14. OVO-VEGETARIANS EAT VEGETABLES, EGGS, AND FISH.

TRUE OR FALSE? → → → →

15. GINGER IS THE MAIN INGREDIENT IN GINGERBREAD COOKIES.

TRUE OR FALSE? ➤ ➤ ➤ ➤

16. APPLES ARE A MEMBER OF THE ROSE FAMILY.

TRUE OR FALSE? → → → →

17. CHIOCCIOLE IS A KIND OF CHOCOLATE.

TRUE OR FALSE? ⇒ ⇒ ⇒ ⇒

See the back of the page to find out.

13. **True.** Some potato varieties are black, white, purple, and other colors.

14. **False.** Ovo-vegetarians eat eggs and vegetables but not meat, fish, or dairy.

15. **False.** Flour is the main ingredient in gingerbread cookies.

16. **True.** Apples, pears, plums, cherries, and strawberries are all related to roses.

17. **False.** Chiocciole is shell-shaped pasta.

18. BOTTLED HOT SAUCE WAS FIRST SOLD IN THE UNITED STATES IN THE 1930s.

TRUE OR FALSE? ⇨ ⇨ ⇨ ⇨

19. CORIANDER AND CILANTRO ARE TWO NAMES FOR THE SAME HERB.

TRUE OR FALSE? ⇒ ⇒ ⇒ ⇒

20. APPLES ARE NATIVE TO THE AMERICAS.

TRUE OR FALSE? → → → →

See the back of the page to find out.

➪ 18. **False.** Bottled hot sauce has been sold in the United States since at least the early 1800s, and Tabasco brand hot sauce has been sold since 1868.

➡ 19. **True.** In North America, coriander is more commonly known as cilantro when it is fresh, and as coriander when sold in seed or ground varieties.

➡ 20. **False.** The first apple seeds came to the Americas with European colonists in the 1600s.

Geography

21. THE LARGEST ISLAND IN THE WORLD IS AUSTRALIA.

TRUE OR FALSE?

22. NEW GUINEA IS THE SECOND LARGEST ISLAND IN THE WORLD.

TRUE OR FALSE?

23. THE SOUTHERNMOST CITY IN THE WORLD IS IN SOUTH AFRICA.

TRUE OR FALSE?

24. THE WORLD'S TALLEST BUILDING IS MORE THAN HALF A MILE HIGH.

TRUE OR FALSE?

25. TEN U.S. STATES HAVE NEVER HAD AN EARTHQUAKE.

TRUE OR FALSE?

See the back of the page to find out.

21. **False.** Australia is technically considered a continent instead of an island. Greenland is the world's largest island.

22. **True.** New Guinea is second to Greenland at about 35 percent of its size.

23. **False.** Puerto Williams in Chile or Ushuaia in Argentina are each sometimes considered the world's southernmost city. Puerto Williams has a much smaller population (just a few thousand people compared to more than 50,000 in Usuaia) but it is further south.

24. **True.** Burj Khalifa in Dubai is 2,722 feet (828 m) high and has 163 floors. There are 5,280 feet in a mile.

25. **False.** Earthquakes are possible in any state. But North Dakota and Florida are the states with the fewest according to the U.S. Geological Survey.

26. THE LARGEST COUNTRY IN THE WORLD BY AREA IS RUSSIA.

TRUE OR FALSE?

27. RUSSIA HAS 15 TIME ZONES.

TRUE OR FALSE?

28. OVER 95 PERCENT OF THE WATER IN THE WORLD IS SALT WATER.

TRUE OR FALSE?

29. IT TAKES 90 DAYS FOR A DROP OF WATER TO TRAVEL THE LENGTH OF THE MISSISSIPPI RIVER.

TRUE OR FALSE?

30. THE NILE RIVER IS THE ONLY RIVER IN THE NORTHERN HEMISPHERE THAT FLOWS SOUTH TO NORTH.

TRUE OR FALSE?

See the back of the page to find out.

26. **True.** Russia's land area is 6.3 million square miles (16.4 million square km), making it the largest country in the world.

27. **False.** Russia has 11 time zones.

28. **True.** Freshwater makes up less than 5 percent of the world's water supply.

29. **True.** A single drop of water would take 90 days to travel from Lake Itasca in Minnesota to the Gulf of Mexico.

30. **False.** There are hundreds of rivers that flow south to north.

31. 25 PERCENT OF THE WORLD'S POPULATION LIVES IN THE SOUTHERN HEMISPHERE.

TRUE OR FALSE?

32. ONE OF THE WORLD'S CAPITAL CITIES IS KRUNG THEP MAHANAKHON AMON RATTANAKOSIN MAHINTHARA YUTHAYA MAHADILOK PHOP NOPPHARAT RATCHATHANI BURIROM UDOMRATCHANIWET MAHASATHAN AMON PIMAN AWATAN SATHIT SAKKATHATTIYA WITSANUKAM PRASIT.

TRUE OR FALSE?

33. THERE ARE NO MOSQUITOES IN ICELAND.

TRUE OR FALSE?

See the back of the page to find out.

➠ 31. **False.** About 10 percent of the world's population lives in the Southern Hemisphere.

➡ 32. **True.** It is more commonly known to English speakers as Bangkok, Thailand, and to Thai speakers as Krung Thep.

✏ 33. **True.** Mosquitoes are found in almost every country in the world except for Iceland.

34. The Hawaiian mountain Mauna Kea is taller from base to peak than Mount Everest.

TRUE OR FALSE? ➤➤ ➤➤ ➤➤ ➤➤

35. Mount Everest is the closest point on Earth to the moon.

TRUE OR FALSE? → → → →

36. Los Angeles, California, is east of Reno, Nevada.

TRUE OR FALSE? ➡ ➡ ➡ ➡

37. The tallest mountain in Europe is in Switzerland.

TRUE OR FALSE? ➤➤ ➤➤ ➤➤ ➤➤

38. Russia and China both border the same number of countries.

TRUE OR FALSE? ⊃ ⊃ ⊃ ⊃

See the back of the page to find out.

➡➤ 34. **True.** From its base at the bottom of the Pacific, Mauna Kea is more than 3,000 feet (1,000 m) taller than Mount Everest. However, Mount Everest is usually considered the tallest mountain because mountain measurements start at sea level.

⟶ 35. **False.** Because the earth is not perfectly round—it bulges just south of the equator—the peak of Mount Chimborazo in Ecuador is about 1.5 miles closer to the moon than Mount Everest's peak.

➡ 36. **True.** The state of Nevada is east of California, but California bends so that Los Angeles is east of Reno.

➤➤➤ 37. **False.** The tallest mountain in Europe is Mount Elbrus in Russia at 18,510 feet (5,642 m).

⟳ 38. **True.** Russia and China both border 14 countries, tying them for the most in the world.

39. THERE ARE FOUR LANDLOCKED COUNTRIES IN THE WORLD COMPLETELY SURROUNDED BY JUST ONE OTHER COUNTRY.

TRUE OR FALSE? ➜ ➜ ➜ ➜

40. THE OLDEST CONTINUOUSLY OCCUPIED CITY IN THE WORLD IS CAIRO, EGYPT.

TRUE OR FALSE? ➤ ➤ ➤ ➤

41. MOST OF THE U.S. COASTLINE IS ON THE ATLANTIC COAST.

TRUE OR FALSE? ➡ ➡ ➡ ➡

42. ISTANBUL IS THE ONLY CITY THAT SPANS TWO CONTINENTS.

TRUE OR FALSE? ⇒ ⇒ ⇒ ⇒

43. THERE ARE MORE THAN 7,000 CARIBBEAN ISLANDS.

TRUE OR FALSE? ⇨ ⇨ ⇨ ⇨

39. **False.** There are three countries completely surrounded by one other country: Lesotho; San Marino; and Vatican City.

40. **False.** Damascus, Syria, is believed to be the oldest continuously occupied city in the world. It has been inhabited for more than 11,000 years.

41. **False.** Most of the U.S. coastline is on the Pacific Coast, the bulk of which is due to Alaska.

42. **False.** Other transcontinental cities include Suez, Egypt, and cities in Russia and Kazakhstan.

43. **True.** More than 7,000 Caribbean islands represent some 26 nations/territories.

44. BRAZIL BORDERS EVERY COUNTRY IN SOUTH AMERICA EXCEPT ONE.

    TRUE OR FALSE?

45. THE LARGEST CITY IN THE UNITED STATES BY AREA IS IN ALASKA.

    TRUE OR FALSE?

46. INDIA HAS THREE TIME ZONES.

    TRUE OR FALSE?

47. A BUILDING CAN HAVE ITS OWN ZIP CODE.

    TRUE OR FALSE?

48. THE CAPITAL OF NEW YORK STATE IS NEW YORK CITY.

    TRUE OR FALSE?

49. KANSAS CITY IS THE CAPITAL OF KANSAS.

    TRUE OR FALSE?

➠ 44. **False.** Neither Ecuador nor Chile border Brazil, which is the largest country in South America.

➜ 45. **True.** Sitka, Alaska, only has a population of 10,000 residents, but it spans more than 2,800 square miles (nearly 12,500 sq km).

✎ 46. **False.** All of India is on one time zone, known as Indian Standard Time. It is 10.5 hours ahead of the U.S.'s Eastern Standard Time.

➻ 47. **True.** There are 42 buildings in New York City that have their own zip codes.

➜ 48. **False.** The capital of New York State is Albany.

➡ 49. **False.** Topeka is the capital of Kansas.

50. ONE COUNTRY HAS OVER 800 LANGUAGES.

TRUE OR FALSE? ⤏ ⤏ ⤏ ⤏

51. IT NEVER SNOWS IN HAWAII.

TRUE OR FALSE? ⊃ ⊃ ⊃ ⊃

52. INDONESIA IS THE WORLD'S LARGEST PRODUCER OF COCONUTS.

TRUE OR FALSE? ➔ ➔ ➔ ➔

➣→ 50. **True.** Approximately 840 living languages are spoken in Papua New Guinea.

⊃ 51. **False.** Several of Hawaii's volcanoes are high enough in elevation that they have snow in winter.

➡ 52. **True.** Indonesia generates more coconuts than any other country in the world.

53. THE SHORTEST RIVER IN THE UNITED STATES IS SHORTER THAN A FOOTBALL FIELD.

TRUE OR FALSE? ➤ ➤ ➤ ➤

54. SWITZERLAND AND GERMANY HAVE THE SAME MOST POPULAR LAST NAME.

TRUE OR FALSE? ➡ ➡ ➡ ➡

55. ANTARCTICA IS A DESERT.

TRUE OR FALSE? ⇒ ⇒ ⇒ ⇒

56. THE NAMES PETROGRAD, LENINGRAD, AND ST. PETERSBURG ALL REFER TO THE SAME RUSSIAN CITY.

TRUE OR FALSE? ⇨ ⇨ ⇨ ⇨

57. PHOENIX, ARIZONA, WAS PREVIOUSLY CALLED CACTUSVILLE.

TRUE OR FALSE? ⟹ ⟹ ⟹ ⟹

> 53. **True.** The Roe River in Montana is just 201 feet (61 m) long.

→ 54. **True.** Müller is the most popular last name in both Switzerland and Germany.

⇒ 55. **True.** Antarctica receives less than 10 inches of rain each year, which makes it a desert.

⇨ 56. **True.** St. Petersburg, the second-largest city in Russia, changed its name to Petrograd from 1914 to 1924 and then Leningrad from 1924 to 1991 before it went back to its earlier name.

⇢ 57. **False.** But before it was a city, some local residents referred to part of the area that would become Phoenix, Arizona, as "Pumpkinville," due to the wild pumpkins that grew there.

58. THE FIRST GAS STATION IN THE UNITED STATES WAS IN DETROIT.

TRUE OR FALSE? → → → →

59. AMERICA'S FIRST ZOO WAS IN PHILADELPHIA.

TRUE OR FALSE? ✏ ✏ ✏ ✏

60. ASIA HAS 7 OF THE WORLD'S 10 MOST POPULATED CITIES.

TRUE OR FALSE? ⇉ ⇉ ⇉ ⇉

See the back of the page to find out.

→ 58. **False.** Pittsburgh claims the honor of being home to the first U.S. drive-in gas station. It opened in 1913.

59. **True.** The Philadelphia Zoological Gardens first opened in 1874 and is still operating today.

➤ 60. **True.** Asia's seven most populous cities are Tokyo, Japan; Delhi, India; Shanghai, China; Dhaka, Bangladesh; Beijing, China; Mumbai, India; and Osaka, Japan.

Human Body

61. THERE ARE 27 BONES IN EACH HAND.

TRUE OR FALSE? → → → →

62. THERE ARE 27 BONES IN EACH FOOT.

TRUE OR FALSE? ➡ ➡ ➡ ➡

63. THE HUMAN HEART BEATS A MAXIMUM OF 50,000 TIMES A DAY.

TRUE OR FALSE? ⇉ ⇉ ⇉ ⇉

64. THE LARGEST HUMAN ORGAN IS THE LIVER.

TRUE OR FALSE? ↻ ↻ ↻ ↻

See the back of the page to find out.

→ 61. **True.** Of the 27 bones in each hand, the smallest bone is the trapezoid bone. It is found not in the little finger but in the palm.

➡ 62. **False.** There are 26 bones in each human foot. More than half of the bones in the human body are found in the hands and feet.

➤ 63. **False.** The human heart beats approximately 100,000 times a day.

⟳ 64. **False.** The largest organ is the skin, but the liver is the largest internal organ.

65. IF YOU LOSE A FINGERNAIL, IT CAN TAKE UP TO SIX MONTHS FOR IT TO GROW BACK.

TRUE OR FALSE? → → → →

year 1 year 2 year 3 year 4 year 5 year 6 year 7 year 8 year 9

66. THE HAIR ON YOUR HEAD GROWS APPROXIMATELY SIX INCHES PER YEAR.

TRUE OR FALSE? ➤ ➤ ➤ ➤

➡ 65. **True.** A fingernail grows an average of 0.13 inches (3.47 mm) per month.

➤ 66. **True.** Hair grows approximately one-half inch per month.

67. TOENAILS GROW AT THE SAME RATE AS FINGERNAILS.

   TRUE OR FALSE? ➡ ➡ ➡ ➡

68. THE BRAIN STAYS THE SAME SIZE FROM BIRTH TO DEATH.

   TRUE OR FALSE? ⟹ ⟹ ⟹ ⟹

69. IF IT WERE PHYSICALLY POSSIBLE TO LAY ALL OF THEM END TO END, ONE PERSON'S BLOOD VESSELS COULD CIRCLE THE GLOBE.

   TRUE OR FALSE? ⇨ ⇨ ⇨ ⇨

70. THE AVERAGE HUMAN HEART WEIGHS LESS THAN A POUND.

   TRUE OR FALSE? ⟫➡ ⟫➡ ⟫➡ ⟫➡

71. THE HUMAN HEART CAN BEAT MORE THAN 3 BILLION TIMES IN A PERSON'S LIFE.

   TRUE OR FALSE? ➡ ➡ ➡ ➡

➡ 67.   **False.** Toenails usually grow at less than half of the rate of fingernails.

⇒ 68.   **False.** The adult brain is more than three times the size of a newborn's brain.

⇨ 69.   **True.** If the average person's blood vessels were laid out, they would extend 60,000 miles (100,000 km), enough to circle Earth twice.

➡ 70.   **True.** The average human heart weighs between 7 and 15 ounces (200 to 450 grams).

➡ 71.   **True.** By the end of a long life, the average human heart has expanded and contracted more than 3.5 billion times.

72. THERE ARE EXACTLY FOUR BLOOD TYPES.

TRUE OR FALSE? ✏ ✏ ✏ ✏

73. WATER MAKES UP ABOUT THREE-QUARTERS OF THE HUMAN BRAIN AND HEART.

TRUE OR FALSE? ➤➤ ➤➤ ➤➤ ➤➤

74. THE BONES ARE COMPOSED OF LESS THAN 25 PERCENT WATER.

TRUE OR FALSE? → → → →

75. YOU HAVE BETWEEN 2 AND 5 MILLION SWEAT GLANDS.

TRUE OR FALSE? ➡ ➡ ➡ ➡

72. **False.** While we are most familiar with the categories A, B, O, and AB, there are around 30 recognized ways to type blood.

73. **True.** The brain and heart are 73 percent water. The lungs are about 83 percent water.

74. **False.** Bones are made up of 31 percent water.

75. **True.** The average person has 2 to 5 million sweat glands—about 200 sweat glands per square inch of skin.

76. THE TALLEST MAN ON RECORD WAS ALMOST 9 FEET TALL.

TRUE OR FALSE?

77. THE HEAVIEST HUMAN ON RECORD WEIGHED MORE THAN 1,000 POUNDS.

TRUE OR FALSE?

See the back of the page to find out.

➤➤→ 76. **True.** Robert Wadlow, born in Illinois in 1918, still holds the record for tallest human, at 8 feet, 11.1 inches (2.72 m) tall.

⟳ 77. **True.** Jon Brower Minnoch, born in Washington State in 1941, at one point weighed 1,400 pounds (635 kg).

78. THE WEAKEST MUSCLE IN THE BODY IS IN THE LITTLE TOE.

TRUE OR FALSE? ➔ ➔ ➔ ➔

79. THE LARGEST MUSCLE IN THE BODY IS THE ONE YOU SIT ON.

TRUE OR FALSE? ➢ ➢ ➢ ➢

80. SOME PEOPLE ARE BORN WITH SIX FINGERS ON EACH HAND.

TRUE OR FALSE? ➡ ➡ ➡ ➡

81. INFANTS AND ADULTS HAVE THE SAME NUMBER OF BONES.

TRUE OR FALSE? ⇒ ⇒ ⇒ ⇒

82. ALL PARTS OF THE HUMAN BODY SHRINK IN OLD AGE.

TRUE OR FALSE? ⇨ ⇨ ⇨ ⇨

See the back of the page to find out.

➡️ 78. **False.** The stapedius muscle in the middle ear is the weakest muscle.

➤ 79. **True.** The largest muscle is the gluteus maximus (butt) muscle.

➡️ 80. **True.** About one in every 700–1,000 people are born with polydactyly—more than five fingers on each hand or five toes on each foot (or both).

⟹ 81. **False.** Infants are born with 300 bones and some fuse together during development. Adults have 206 bones.

⇨ 82. **False.** While much of the body gets smaller with old age (post adulthood), the nose and ears are made of cartilage and keep getting bigger due to the pull of gravity on the flexible tissue.

83. THE GUINNESS WORLD RECORD HOLDER FOR OLDEST PERSON (WITH AGE DOCUMENTATION) DIED IN 1997 AT OVER 122 YEARS OLD.

TRUE OR FALSE? ⇒ ⇒ ⇒ ⇒

84. IT IS POSSIBLE TO BE BORN WITH TWO DIFFERENT COLORED EYES.

TRUE OR FALSE? → → → →

85. THE LUNGS ARE NATURALLY BLUE IN COLOR.

TRUE OR FALSE? ✏ ✏ ✏ ✏

86. SKIN CAN BE HOME TO MORE THAN 1,000 DIFFERENT BACTERIA SPECIES.

TRUE OR FALSE? ➤ ➤ ➤ ➤

87. TOGETHER, THE SMALL AND LARGE INTESTINES ARE ABOUT 50 FEET (15.25 M) IN LENGTH.

TRUE OR FALSE? → → → →

See the back of the page to find out.

➠ 83. **True.** Jeanne Calment of Arles, France, had evidence showing that she was 122 years and 164 days old when she died, but some of that evidence has been questioned in recent years.

➡ 84. **True.** The condition of having eyes in two different colors is called heterochromia iridum.

✏ 85. **False.** Lungs are made of a soft, pink spongy tissue.

➤➤ 86. **True.** The presence of bacteria on and in humans is probably essential to bodies working properly.

➡ 87. **False.** The small and large intestine total about 15 to 25 feet (3 to 7.5 m) in length.

88. THE HUMAN BRAIN IS BIGGER THAN YOU MIGHT EXPECT IN A MAMMAL OF ITS SIZE.

TRUE OR FALSE? ➡ ➡ ➡ ➡

89. THE HUMAN SKULL IS ONE BONE.

TRUE OR FALSE? ➤ ➤ ➤ ➤

90. THE RIGHT SIDE OF THE HUMAN BRAIN CONTROLS THE LEFT SIDE OF THE BODY.

TRUE OR FALSE? ⟩ ⟩ ⟩ ⟩

91. THE BRAIN IS MOSTLY MADE UP OF FAT.

TRUE OR FALSE? ➔ ➔ ➔ ➔

92. THE HUMAN BRAIN CONTAINS ABOUT 100 BILLION NEURONS (NERVE CELLS THAT TRANSMIT INFORMATION).

TRUE OR FALSE? ➢ ➢ ➢ ➢

88. **True.** The human brain is about three times the size of the brain in other mammals. Humans have a brain-to-bodyweight ratio of 1-to-50. Most mammals have a ratio of 1-to-180.

89. **False.** The human skull consists of 22 interconnected bones.

90. **True.** Each side of the human brain interacts with the muscles and glands on the other side.

91. **True.** Sixty percent of the human brain's weight is from fat.

92. **True.** Neurons are the basic unit of the brain and nervous system.

93. THE BRAIN TAKES UP LESS THAN 10 PERCENT OF THE HUMAN BODY'S TOTAL ENERGY USE.

TRUE OR FALSE? ➡ ➡ ➡ ➡

94. YOUR EPIDERMIS IS SHOWING.

TRUE OR FALSE? ⇒ ⇒ ⇒ ⇒

95. RED BLOOD CELLS FIGHT INFECTION.

TRUE OR FALSE? ⇨ ⇨ ⇨ ⇨

96. AN AVERAGE HUMAN BODY HAS 30 TRILLION CELLS.

TRUE OR FALSE? ⇶ ⇶ ⇶ ⇶

97. WHITE BLOOD CELLS ARE ABOUT 50 PERCENT OF THE CELLS IN HUMAN BLOOD.

TRUE OR FALSE? ➡ ➡ ➡ ➡

See the back of the page to find out.

➡ 93. **False.** The human brain uses about 20 percent of the body's energy— more than any other organ.

⟹ 94. **True.** The epidermis is the outermost of the three layers of skin, so part of it is probably always showing!

⟹ 95. **False.** Red blood cells carry oxygen from the lungs to the rest of the body and then make a return trip, bringing carbon dioxide back to the lungs to be exhaled. White blood cells fight infections.

⟹ 96. **True.** The average human body has 30,000,000,000,000 cells.

➡ 97. **False.** White blood cells account for only about 1 percent of human blood volume.

98. THE HUMAN BRAIN HAS THE POTENTIAL TO READ ALMOST 1,000 WORDS A MINUTE.

TRUE OR FALSE?

99. CROSSING YOUR ARMS CAN REDUCE PAIN.

TRUE OR FALSE?

100. YOU CAN'T TICKLE YOURSELF.

TRUE OR FALSE?

See the back of the page to find out.

98. **True.** But while the human brain is technically capable of processing 1,000 words a minute, most people average about 200.

99. **True.** A study in 2011 showed that crossing the arms at the wrist confused the perception of pain signals in the brain.

100. **True.** Because your brain predicts the movement, and the element of surprise is a big part of what makes you ticklish, you can't tickle yourself.

Living Things

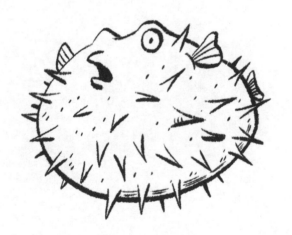

101. THE AGE OF A TREE CAN BE DETERMINED BY THE NUMBER OF RINGS.

TRUE OR FALSE? ➡ ➡ ➡ ➡

102. ASPIRIN WAS FIRST DERIVED FROM PINE TREES.

TRUE OR FALSE? ⟫→ ⟫→ ⟫→ ⟫→

103. A SUNFLOWER IS HUNDREDS OF TINY FLOWERS.

TRUE OR FALSE? ⊃ ⊃ ⊃ ⊃

104. TREES ARE THE LONGEST LIVING ORGANISMS ON EARTH.

TRUE OR FALSE? → → → →

105. ALL PLANTS HAVE ROOTS THAT GROW INTO THE GROUND.

TRUE OR FALSE? ➤ ➤ ➤ ➤

See the back of the page to find out.

101. **True.** Aging a tree by counting the rings is called dendrochronology.

102. **False.** An early form of aspirin was first found in willow tree leaves.

103. **True.** A sunflower is made up of hundreds of florets.

104. **True.** A Great Basin bristlecone pine in California's White Mountains is over 5,000 years old.

105. **False.** Epiphytes are plants that grow on other plants and have no roots.

106. MOST CACTI ARE NATURALLY COVERED WITH A WAXY COATING.

TRUE OR FALSE? ➡ ➡ ➡ ➡

107. ALL OAK TREES PRODUCE ACORNS.

TRUE OR FALSE? ⇒ ⇒ ⇒ ⇒

108. THE MOSQUITO IS THE DEADLIEST ANIMAL ON THE PLANET.

TRUE OR FALSE? ⇨ ⇨ ⇨ ⇨

109. THE CASSOWARY BIRD CAN RUN UP TO 31 MILES PER HOUR.

TRUE OR FALSE? ⇥ ⇥ ⇥ ⇥

See the back of the page to find out.

➡ 106. **True.** The waxy surface on cacti keeps water from evaporating.

⟹ 107. **False.** Most oak trees don't produce acorns until they are about 20 years old.

⇨ 108. **True.** Mosquitoes can carry diseases like malaria that have killed millions of people.

➡ 109. **True.** The cassowary bird cannot fly but it can run up to 31 miles (50 km) per hour.

110. A HYENA CAN EAT AN ENTIRE ZEBRA IN LESS THAN HALF AN HOUR.

TRUE OR FALSE?

I couldn't eat a whole one.

111. A PENGUIN'S BLACK AND WHITE COLORS ARE FOR CAMOUFLAGE.

TRUE OR FALSE?

112. ALL BIRDS LAY EGGS IN THE SPRING.

TRUE OR FALSE?

→ 110. **False.** Hyenas can consume up to one-third of their body weight in one meal, but zebras are still too big to be eaten by just one hyena.

✏ 111. **True.** A penguin's black and white colors help them hide from predators underwater.

➡ 112. **False.** Emperor penguins lay their eggs in the winter, not in the spring.

113. Birds can be poisonous.

TRUE OR FALSE? → → → →

114. Fish can be poisonous.

TRUE OR FALSE? ➡ ➡ ➡ ➡

115. The largest reptile is the Komodo dragon.

TRUE OR FALSE? ⇢ ⇢ ⇢ ⇢

116. The temperature in a beehive is constant.

TRUE OR FALSE? ⊃ ⊃ ⊃ ⊃

See the back of the page to find out.

→ 113. **True.** The skin and feathers of the hooded pitohui, native to Papua New Guinea, contain a neurotoxin that makes them poisonous to touch or eat.

➡ 114. **True.** Pufferfish create the poison tetrodotoxin that is up to 1,200 times more deadly to humans than cyanide.

⇉ 115. **False.** The largest reptile is the saltwater crocodile, which can weigh up to 2,200 pounds (1,000 kg).

⊃ 116. **True.** Bees try to keep the temperature in a beehive to a steady 90–95 degrees Fahrenheit and rarely allow it to shift more than 1 or 2 degrees in a 24-hour period.

117. THE SALUKI IS THE ONE OF THE WORLD'S OLDEST DOG BREEDS.

TRUE OR FALSE? → → → →

118. THOUSANDS OF PEOPLE KEEP TIGERS AS PETS.

TRUE OR FALSE? ➤ ➤ ➤ ➤

119. THE MOST POPULAR DOG BREED IS THE GOLDEN RETRIEVER.

TRUE OR FALSE? → → → →

See the back of the page to find out.

➡ *117.* **True.** The Saluki breed traces its roots back several thousand years, to the Fertile Crescent region.

➤ *118.* **True.** An estimated 6,000 tigers are kept as pets in the United States, even though it is illegal in many states.

➡ *119.* **False.** The most registered dog breed in the United States is the Labrador Retriever.

120. Koi fish can live hundreds of years.

TRUE OR FALSE? ⇒ ⇒ ⇒ ⇒

121. Oysters can change their sex.

TRUE OR FALSE? ⇨ ⇨ ⇨ ⇨

122. There are only 12 species of sharks.

TRUE OR FALSE? ⇢ ⇢ ⇢ ⇢

123. A spider has a small brain.

TRUE OR FALSE? → → → →

124. All birds can only navigate during the day.

TRUE OR FALSE? ⬤➤ ⬤➤ ⬤➤ ⬤➤

125. Butterflies are colorblind.

TRUE OR FALSE? ➤➤ ➤➤ ➤➤ ➤➤

See the back of the page to find out.

⟹ 120. **True.** The oldest known koi was believed to have lived 226 years.

⇨ 121. **True.** Oysters can change from male to female and back again.

⮕ 122. **False.** There are more than 500 species of sharks.

→ 123. **False.** The brains of some spiders are so large that they expand into the body cavity and even into the legs.

✏ 124. **False.** Scientists in the 1960s identified how the indigo bunting navigates at night using the stars.

➡ 125. **False.** Butterflies have complex color vision and can even see in the ultraviolet range.

126. NEWBORN KANGAROOS ARE SMALLER THAN A BASEBALL.

TRUE OR FALSE? → → → →

127. SONG SPARROWS' HEARTS BEAT FASTER THAN HUMAN HEARTS.

TRUE OR FALSE? ➡ ➡ ➡ ➡

128. TASMANIAN DEVILS' EARS CAN CHANGE COLOR.

TRUE OR FALSE? ⧦ ⧦ ⧦ ⧦

129. A WOMBAT'S POUCH OPENS AT THE TOP, AT ITS CHEST.

TRUE OR FALSE? ⊃ ⊃ ⊃ ⊃

130. A WORM CAN GROW TO MORE THAN 100 FEET LONG.

TRUE OR FALSE? → → → →

→ 126. **True.** A newborn kangaroo is about the size of a peanut shell.

➡ 127. **True.** A song sparrow's heart can beat over 500 times a minute. Human hearts average 60–100 beats per minute.

➤➤➤ 128. **True.** The ears of a Tasmanian devil turn bright red when they are scared or agitated.

⟳ 129. **False.** A wombat's pouch opens at the bottom.

➡ 130. **True.** The bootlace worm has been known to grow to 150 feet long.

131. SOME FISH DON'T HAVE EYES.

TRUE OR FALSE? ➤ ➤ ➤ ➤

132. SOME FISH CAN LAY MILLIONS OF EGGS AT A TIME.

TRUE OR FALSE? ➤ ➤ ➤ ➤

See the back of the page to find out.   71

➤ 131.   **True.** Some cave-dwelling fish, such as the Mexican tetra, have evolved to not have eyes.

➤ 132.   **True.** The ocean sunfish can lay 300 million eggs at a time.

Pop Culture

133. VIDEO GAME COMPANY NINTENDO WAS FOUNDED IN 1889.

TRUE OR FALSE? ⇒ ⇒ ⇒ ⇒

134. WALT DISNEY DIDN'T KNOW HOW DRAW WHEN HE STARTED HIS ANIMATION COMPANY.

TRUE OR FALSE? ⇨ ⇨ ⇨ ⇨

135. WALT DISNEY HAS RECEIVED MORE OSCARS (ACADEMY AWARDS) THAN ANYONE ELSE IN HISTORY.

TRUE OR FALSE? ⇛ ⇛ ⇛ ⇛

136. THE ORIGINAL *TOY STORY* MOVIE WAS THE FIRST FULL-LENGTH FEATURE FILM TO BE COMPUTER ANIMATED.

TRUE OR FALSE? → → → →

⇒ 133. **True.** Nintendo was founded in Japan in 1889 to make playing cards.

⇨ 134. **False.** Walt Disney started drawing when he was four years old.

⇒ 135. **True.** Walt Disney received 22 Academy Awards.

→ 136. **True.** *Toy Story* was the first full-length film made entirely using computer animation. It was also the first Pixar film.

137. *THE LORD OF THE RINGS* HAS SOLD MORE COPIES AS A SINGLE-VOLUME BOOK THAN THE ENTIRE HARRY POTTER SERIES.

TRUE OR FALSE?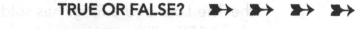

138. BILLIE EILISH IS THE YOUNGEST WINNER OF THE GRAMMY AWARD FOR RECORD OF THE YEAR.

TRUE OR FALSE?

✏ 137. **False.** In 2018, it was estimated that the *The Lord of the Rings* has sold about 150 million copies, compared with 500 million Harry Potter books.

➤➤ 138. **True.** Billie Eilish also won the award for album of the year in 2020 at age 18.

139. Mark Zuckerberg, who started Facebook, and Bill Gates, who started Microsoft, both graduated from Harvard.

TRUE OR FALSE? → → → →

140. Star Wars day is May 4.

TRUE OR FALSE? ⮕ ⮕ ⮕ ⮕

141. Justin Bieber is Canadian.

TRUE OR FALSE? ⯈ ⯈ ⯈ ⯈

142. The first costumed comic superhero was Superman.

TRUE OR FALSE? ↻ ↻ ↻ ↻

143. Stan Lee created X-Men.

TRUE OR FALSE? ⇢ ⇢ ⇢ ⇢

See the back of the page to find out. 79

Answers for previous page.

→ *139.* **False.** Zuckerberg and Gates both attended Harvard but never graduated.

➡ *140.* **True.** May the "fourth" be with you.

⇶ *141.* **True.** Justin Bieber was born in London, Ontario, Canada in 1994.

⟳ *142.* **False.** The Phantom debuted as the first superhero in newspaper comic strips in 1936, two years before the first Superman comic book.

⟾ *143.* **True.** Stan Lee and Jack Kirby created X-Men for Marvel Comics in 1963.

144. KRYPTONITE IS BLUE.

TRUE OR FALSE? ➔ ➔ ➔ ➔

145. *MINECRAFT* IS THE BESTSELLING VIDEO GAME OF ALL TIME.

TRUE OR FALSE? ➢ ➢ ➢ ➢

146. THERE ARE NINE DIFFERENT TYPES OF PUZZLE PIECES IN THE VIDEO GAME *TETRIS*.

TRUE OR FALSE? ➔ ➔ ➔ ➔

147. KELLY CLARKSON BECAME FAMOUS WHEN SHE WON *AMERICA'S GOT TALENT*.

TRUE OR FALSE? ⇒ ⇒ ⇒ ⇒

See the back of the page to find out.

➡ 144. **False.** Kryptonite, which makes Superman powerless, is green.

➤ 145. **True.** *Minecraft* has sold more than 200 million copies since it was released in 2011.

➡ 146. **False.** There are seven pieces, known as "tetriminos" in *Tetris*.

⟹ 147. **False.** Kelly Clarkson was the first winner of *American Idol*.

148. Future President Donald Trump appeared in the first *Home Alone* movie in 1990.

TRUE OR FALSE? ⇨ ⇨ ⇨ ⇨

149. Former President Barack Obama collects comic books.

TRUE OR FALSE? ⇒ ⇒ ⇒ ⇒

150. Videos recorded using the TikTok app can be up to three minutes long.

TRUE OR FALSE? → → → →

151. The singer Usher's real first name is Usher.

TRUE OR FALSE? ✏ ✏ ✏ ✏

152. Chance the Rapper's real first name is Chancelor.

TRUE OR FALSE? ➤ ➤ ➤ ➤

See the back of the page to find out.

➡️ 148.   **False.** Donald Trump appeared in *Home Alone 2*.

➡️ 149.   **True.** President Obama has a collection of Spider-Man and Conan the Barbarian comics.

➡️ 150.   **False.** The maximum length of TikTok videos is 60 seconds.

✏️ 151.   **True.** Usher was born Usher Raymond IV.

➤➤ 152.   **True.** Chance the Rapper was born Chancelor Jonathan Bennett in Chicago in 1993.

84

153. TESLA FOUNDER ELON MUSK AND SINGER GRIMES GAVE THEIR SON THE NAME X Æ A-12.

TRUE OR FALSE? → → → →

154. THE CHARACTERS OF DARTH VADER IN THE STAR WARS FILMS AND MUFASA IN THE ORIGINAL *THE LION KING* MOVIE ARE VOICED BY THE SAME ACTOR.

TRUE OR FALSE? ➡ ➡ ➡ ➡

155. BUGS BUNNY, DAFFY DUCK, AND PORKY PIG WERE ALL ORIGINALLY VOICED BY THE SAME ACTOR.

TRUE OR FALSE? ⤖ ⤖ ⤖ ⤖

156. LOVE-30 IS THE NAME OF A ROBOT CHARACTER IN *STAR WARS*.

TRUE OR FALSE? ⊃ ⊃ ⊃ ⊃

See the back of the page to find out. 85

Answers for previous page.

→ 153. **True.** The unusual name X Æ A-12 is pronounced "X Ash A 12."

➡ 154. **True.** Actor James Earl Jones played voices in both the original Star Wars trilogy and *The Lion King*.

⟫→ 155. **True.** Mel Blanc played the voices of Bugs Bunny, Daffy Duck, Porky Pig, and many other Looney Tunes characters. Blanc was also the voice of Barney Rubble on *The Flintstones*.

⟳ 156. **False.** There is no robot character named Love-30. Love-30 can be a tennis score.

157. ONE ACTOR VOICES BOTH HOMER AND MARGE SIMPSON ON *THE SIMPSONS*.

TRUE OR FALSE? → → → →

158. JUSTIN TIMBERLAKE GOT HIS START IN SHOW BUSINESS BY SINGING AT AMUSEMENT PARKS.

TRUE OR FALSE? ➤ ➤ ➤ ➤

159. *THE SIMPSONS* TAKES PLACE IN SPRINGFIELD, ILLINOIS.

TRUE OR FALSE? ➡ ➡ ➡ ➡

160. ATLANTA IS KNOWN AS THE BIRTHPLACE OF HIP-HOP.

TRUE OR FALSE? ⇒ ⇒ ⇒ ⇒

161. DARTH VADER SAYS "LUKE, I AM YOUR FATHER," IN *STAR WARS: EPISODE 5 – THE EMPIRE STRIKES BACK*.

TRUE OR FALSE? ⇨ ⇨ ⇨ ⇨

➡ 157. **False.** Dan Castellaneta voices Homer Simpson and Julie Kavner voices Marge Simpson.

➤ 158. **False.** Justin Timberlake started to become famous on TV's *The All-New Mickey Mouse Club*, with costars Christina Aguilera, Ryan Gosling, Keri Russell, and Britney Spears.

➡ 159. **False.** *The Simpsons* takes place in the town of Springfield, but the state is never specified.

⇒ 160. **False.** The Bronx, New York, is known as the birthplace of hip-hop.

⇨ 161. **False.** Darth Vader's exact words were, "No, I am your father."

162. THE MOVIE *JAWS* IS ABOUT A KILLER WHALE.

TRUE OR FALSE?

You know, more people are killed by their lawnmowers than by sharks.

See the back of the page to find out.

162. THE MOVIE *JAWS* IS ABOUT A KILLER
WHALE.

TRUE OR FALSE?

➡ *162.* **False.** *Jaws* is about a great white
shark.

90

163. THE SETTING IN MARVEL'S *BLACK PANTHER* IS THE FICTIONAL NATION OF WAKANDA.

TRUE OR FALSE? → → → →

164. JAY PRITCHETT IS A CHARACTER IN THE TV SITCOM *THE OFFICE*.

TRUE OR FALSE? ✎ ✎ ✎ ✎

165. YOSHI IS A CHARACTER IN *SUPER MARIO WORLD*.

TRUE OR FALSE? ➡ ➡ ➡ ➡

166. THE FIRST *POKÉMON* VIDEO GAMES WERE RELEASED IN 2006.

TRUE OR FALSE? → → → →

167. THE MAIN CHARACTER IN *THE LION KING*, SIMBA, WAS GIVEN THAT NAME BECAUSE IT IS THE SWAHILI WORD FOR "LION."

TRUE OR FALSE? ➡ ➡ ➡ ➡

→ 163. **True.** Wakanda was first mentioned in *Fantastic Four* in 1966.

✏ 164. **False.** Jay Pritchett is the name of a character in the sitcom *Modern Family*.

↠ 165. **True.** Yoshi is a dinosaur and sidekick to Luigi and Mario.

⟶ 166. **False.** The first *Pokémon* video games were released in 1996 in Japan and in 1998 in the United States.

➡ 167. **True.** "Simba" is the Swahili word for "lion."

168. Tommie, Chuckie, and Angelica are *Teenage Mutant Ninja Turtles* characters.

TRUE OR FALSE? ⫸→ ⫸→ ⫸→ ⫸→

169. The program *Sesame Street* is more than 50 years old.

TRUE OR FALSE? ⊃ ⊃ ⊃ ⊃

170. Pixar's second feature-length movie was *Toy Story 2*.

TRUE OR FALSE? → → → →

171. The members of 1960s rock band The Beatles all came from London, England.

TRUE OR FALSE? ➢ ➢ ➢ ➢

172. *The Phantom Menace* was the first Star Wars film ever released.

TRUE OR FALSE? ➡ ➡ ➡ ➡

See the back of the page to find out.

168. **False.** Tommie, Chuckie, and Angelica are characters in *Rugrats*.

169. **True.** *Sesame Street* was first broadcast in 1969.

170. **False.** The second full-length Pixar movie was *A Bug's Life*.

171. **False.** All four of the members of The Beatles were born in Liverpool, England.

172. **False.** While *The Phantom Menace* is "Episode I" in the Star Wars saga, the first Star Wars film released was actually *Episode IV – A New Hope* in 1977.

173. ROCK SINGER ELVIS PRESLEY WAS NATURALLY BLOND.

TRUE OR FALSE? ⟹ ⟹ ⟹ ⟹

174. DR. SPOCK WAS A CHARACTER ON *STAR TREK*.

TRUE OR FALSE? ⇨ ⇨ ⇨ ⇨

175. THE TALLEST ROLLER COASTER IN THE WORLD IS THE KINGDA KA.

TRUE OR FALSE? ➠ ➠ ➠ ➠

176. BARBIE'S FULL NAME IS BARBARA MILLICENT ROBERTS.

TRUE OR FALSE? → → → →

177. SIX 8-STUD LEGO BRICKS CAN BE COMBINED IN OVER A MILLION COMBINATIONS.

TRUE OR FALSE? ✏ ✏ ✏ ✏

See the back of the page to find out.

⇒ *173.* **True.** Elvis Presley began dying his hair darker colors as a teenager.

⇨ *174.* **False.** Dr. Benjamin Spock was a famous pediatrician. Mr. Spock was a character on *Star Trek*.

⇒ *175.* **True.** The Kingda Ka coaster in Jackson, New Jersey, is more than 45 stories high.

➔ *176.* **True.** Barbie was named after creator Ruth Handler's daughter, Barbara, and first went on sale in 1959.

⇨ *177.* **True.** A Danish math professor became known for creating a computer program that calculated there are 915,103,765 ways to combine six 8-stud Lego bricks.

178. PLAY-DOH WAS ORIGINALLY INVENTED TO MAKE POTTERY.

TRUE OR FALSE? ➥ ➥ ➥ ➥

179. THE SAME ACTOR WAS THE ORIGINAL VOICE FOR BOTH YODA AND MISS PIGGY.

TRUE OR FALSE? → → → →

➤➤ *178.* **False.** Play-Doh was originally
invented to clean wallpaper.

➤ *179.* **True.** Frank Oz was the original voice
for Yoda and Miss Piggy. He also
performed the characters of Bert,
Cookie Monster, and Grover on
Sesame Street for a time.

Presidents

180. GEORGE WASHINGTON BECAME PRESIDENT ON JULY 4, 1776.

TRUE OR FALSE?

181. PHILADELPHIA WAS ONCE THE CAPITAL OF THE UNITED STATES.

TRUE OR FALSE?

182. AS A YOUNG MAN, ABRAHAM LINCOLN WAS A TALENTED WRESTLER.

TRUE OR FALSE? ⊃ ⊃ ⊃ ⊃

➡ 180. **False.** There was no president of the United States in 1776. George Washington was sworn in as the first president on April 30, 1789.

⇛ 181. **True.** Philadelphia was the capital between 1790 and 1800.

⊃ 182. **True.** It is said that Abraham Lincoln won 199 of 200 wrestling matches, though no official records exist.

183. ABRAHAM LINCOLN NEVER LOST AN ELECTION.

TRUE OR FALSE? ➜ ➜ ➜ ➜

184. THE WHITE HOUSE RESIDENCE HAS 132 ROOMS.

TRUE OR FALSE? ➤ ➤ ➤ ➤

185. THE WHITE HOUSE WAS NOT CALLED THE WHITE HOUSE UNTIL 1901.

TRUE OR FALSE? ➡ ➡ ➡ ➡

186. RUTHERFORD B. HAYES WAS THE FIRST PRESIDENT TO HAVE A TELEPHONE.

TRUE OR FALSE? ⇒ ⇒ ⇒ ⇒

187. GERALD FORD WAS ELECTED PRESIDENT IN 1974.

TRUE OR FALSE? ⇨ ⇨ ⇨ ⇨

➔ *183.* **False.** Lincoln lost several elections, including an 1858 race for a seat in the U.S. Senate, before he was elected president.

➤ *184.* **True.** The White House has 132 rooms and 35 bathrooms on 6 levels.

➔ *185.* **True.** Until 1901, the White House was called the "President's Palace," the "President's House," or the "Executive Mansion."

⇒ *186.* **True.** President Hayes's telephone number was 1.

⇨ *187.* **False.** Gerald Ford was never elected president. He became vice president after the resignation of Vice President Spiro Agnew in 1973 and president after the resignation of President Richard Nixon in 1974.

188. WOODROW WILSON'S FACE IS ON THE $1,000 BILL.

TRUE OR FALSE?

189. THE MIDDLE INITIAL IN ULYSSES S. GRANT STANDS FOR STEVEN.

TRUE OR FALSE?

190. THE MIDDLE INITIAL IN HARRY S. TRUMAN STANDS FOR STEVEN.

TRUE OR FALSE?

191. JOHN F. KENNEDY WAS THE FIRST CATHOLIC PRESIDENT.

TRUE OR FALSE?

192. ONE PRESIDENT NEVER WENT TO SCHOOL.

TRUE OR FALSE?

➠ 188. **False.** Woodrow Wilson's face is on the $100,000 bill.

→ 189. **False.** The "S" in Ulysses S. Grant doesn't stand for anything.

✐ 190. **False.** The "S" in Harry S. Truman doesn't stand for anything.

➤ 191. **True.** John F. Kennedy was the first Catholic president. Joe Biden is the second Catholic president.

→ 192. **True.** Andrew Johnson came from a very poor family and never attended a formal school.

193. A POLICE OFFICER GAVE ULYSSES S. GRANT A SPEEDING TICKET WHILE GRANT WAS SERVING AS PRESIDENT.

TRUE OR FALSE? ➡ ➡ ➡ ➡

194. FRANKLIN D. ROOSEVELT WAS ELECTED PRESIDENT FIVE TIMES.

TRUE OR FALSE? ➤ ➤ ➤ ➤

195. ALEXANDER HAMILTON WAS THE FOURTH U.S. PRESIDENT.

TRUE OR FALSE? ⊃ ⊃ ⊃ ⊃

196. RICHARD NIXON WAS IMPEACHED.

TRUE OR FALSE? → → → →

197. HARRY S. TRUMAN PLAYED THE PIANO.

TRUE OR FALSE? ➢ ➢ ➢ ➢

➡ 193. **True.** Grant received a ticket for driving his horse-drawn buggy too fast.

⇉➡ 194. **False.** Franklin D. Roosevelt was elected president four times.

⊃ 195. **False.** Alexander Hamilton was never president.

➡ 196. **False.** Richard Nixon resigned before he was impeached.

➤ 197. **True.** On the first-ever televised tour of the White House in 1954, Harry S. Truman played Mozart's A Major Sonata.

198. MORE PRESIDENTS WERE BORN IN VIRGINIA THAN ANY OTHER STATE.

TRUE OR FALSE? ➡ ➡ ➡ ➡

199. THE HOUSE OF REPRESENTATIVES DETERMINED THE OUTCOME OF TWO PRESIDENTIAL ELECTIONS.

TRUE OR FALSE? ⇒ ⇒ ⇒ ⇒

200. JOHN F. KENNEDY WAS THE FIRST PRESIDENT BORN IN A HOSPITAL.

TRUE OR FALSE? ⇨ ⇨ ⇨ ⇨

See the back of the page to find out.

→ 198. **True.** Eight U.S. presidents were born in Virginia, including four of the first five presidents.

⇒ 199. **True.** The presidential elections of 1800 and 1824 were decided by a vote in the House of Representatives since no candidate had enough electoral votes.

⇨ 200. **False.** Jimmy Carter was the first president born in a hospital.

201. THE FIRST WOMAN CANDIDATE FOR PRESIDENT CAMPAIGNED FOR THE NATION'S HIGHEST OFFICE IN 1872.

TRUE OR FALSE? ⟹ ⟹ ⟹ ⟹

202. WILLIAM HENRY HARRISON STUDIED TO BE A LAWYER.

TRUE OR FALSE? → → → →

➠ *201.* **True.** In 1872, Victoria Woodhull ran for president as the nominee of the newly formed Equal Rights Party.

→ *202.* **False.** William Henry Harrison briefly studied medicine before leaving school to join the military.

Science

203. ALL OF THE PLANETS IN EARTH'S SOLAR SYSTEM SPIN CLOCKWISE ON THEIR AXES.

TRUE OR FALSE?

204. A FLEA CAN ACCELERATE FASTER THAN NASA'S SPACE SHUTTLES COULD.

TRUE OR FALSE?

See the back of the page to find out.

203. **False.** Venus is the only planet that spins clockwise.

204. **True.** Fleas can accelerate at 100 times the earth's gravity while the Space Shuttle "only" accelerated at five times the earth's gravity.

205. MOST OF EARTH'S OXYGEN IS PRODUCED BY THE RAINFORESTS.

TRUE OR FALSE? → → → →

206. CLOUDS ARE NEARLY WEIGHTLESS.

TRUE OR FALSE? ➡ ➡ ➡ ➡

207. THERE ARE MORE STARS IN THE MILKY WAY GALAXY THAN THERE ARE TREES ON EARTH.

TRUE OR FALSE? ⇉ ⇉ ⇉ ⇉

208. BANANAS ARE RADIOACTIVE.

TRUE OR FALSE? ⊃ ⊃ ⊃ ⊃

209. OXYGEN CAN BE A PALE BLUE COLOR.

TRUE OR FALSE? → → → →

210. SALT WATER FREEZES AT 32 DEGREES FAHRENHEIT.

TRUE OR FALSE? ➢ ➢ ➢ ➢

See the back of the page to find out.

→ 205. **False.** Oceans account for over half of Earth's oxygen production.

➡ 206. **False.** A cumulus cloud can have up to a million pounds of water droplet weight.

⇶→ 207. **False.** It is estimated that there are between 100 billion and 400 billion stars in our galaxy but an estimated 3 trillion trees on Earth.

⊃ 208. **True.** Bananas contain potassium that is very, very slightly radioactive.

➡ 209. **True.** As a gas, oxygen is odorless and colorless, but when it is in liquid or frozen form, it looks pale blue.

➤ 210. **False.** While water freezes at 32 degrees Fahrenheit, salt water freezes at a lower temperature.

211. WATER EXPANDS WHEN IT FREEZES.

      TRUE OR FALSE? → → → →

212. IT CAN RAIN DIAMONDS.

      TRUE OR FALSE? ⇒ ⇒ ⇒ ⇒

213. THE WIND IS SILENT.

      TRUE OR FALSE? ⇨ ⇨ ⇨ ⇨

214. THERE IS NO WIND IN ANTARCTICA.

      TRUE OR FALSE? ⇥ ⇥ ⇥ ⇥

215. MOST OF THE PHYSICAL WORLD
IS EMPTY SPACE.

      TRUE OR FALSE? → → → →

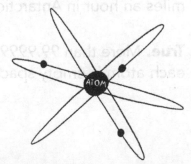

See the back of the page to find out.

→ 211. **True.** Water expands by about nine percent when it goes from its liquid to solid (frozen) state.

⇒ 212. **True.** The atmospheres of Neptune, Uranus, Jupiter, and Saturn have such extreme pressure that scientists believe they can crystallize carbon atoms, creating "diamond rain."

⇨ 213. **True.** Wind only makes noise when it blows against or through something.

⇒ 214. **False.** Winds can blow up to 200 miles an hour in Antarctica.

→ 215. **True.** More than 99.99999 percent of each atom is empty space.

216. THE SURFACE OF THE SUN IS HOTTER THAN THE EARTH'S CORE.

TRUE OR FALSE?

217. LIGHTNING CAN BE HOTTER THAN THE SUN.

TRUE OR FALSE?

218. THE MOON HAS STRONG WINDS.

TRUE OR FALSE?

219. GLASS IS MADE OF SAND.

TRUE OR FALSE?

220. EARTH'S MOON CAN ONLY BE SEEN AT NIGHT.

TRUE OR FALSE?

🖉 *216.* **False.** The temperature of the earth's core is approximately 7,500 Kelvin (the temperature scale used by most scientists). The sun's surface temperature is estimated at less than 6,000 Kelvin.

➤➤ *217.* **True.** NASA estimates that lightning on Earth can be 4 to 6 times hotter than the surface of the sun.

→ *218.* **False.** There is no wind on the moon.

➡ *219.* **True.** If you heat sand, which is mostly made of silicon dioxide, to 3,090 degrees Fahrenheit (1700 Celsius), it will melt into liquid and then become glass when it cools.

⫸➤ *220.* **False.** The earth's revolution on its axis means that the moon is above the horizon for about 12 hours out of every day. It is harder to see the moon when the sky is brightened by the sun, but it can still sometimes be seen during the day.

221. NO PIECE OF PAPER CAN BE FOLDED IN HALF MORE THAN SEVEN TIMES.

    TRUE OR FALSE? ⊃ ⊃ ⊃ ⊃

222. THE PLANETS ARE ALL NAMED AFTER GREEK AND ROMAN GODS.

    TRUE OR FALSE? → → → →

223. COLD WATER AND HOT WATER WEIGH THE SAME.

    TRUE OR FALSE? ➤ ➤ ➤ ➤

221. **False.** In 2002, high school junior Britney Gallivan demonstrated how a 4,000 foot (1,200 m) sheet of toilet paper could be folded in half 12 times.

222. **False.** Earth is the only planet not named after a Greek or Roman god.

223. **False.** Cold water weighs slightly more than hot water if the two amounts are equal in volume.

224. YOU COULD PROBABLY DUNK A BASKETBALL ON MARS.

TRUE OR FALSE? ➔ ➔ ➔ ➔

225. A YEAR ON MARS IS AS LONG AS THREE EARTH YEARS.

TRUE OR FALSE? ⇒ ⇒ ⇒ ⇒

226. SNOW IS WHITE.

TRUE OR FALSE? ⇨ ⇨ ⇨ ⇨

See the back of the page to find out.

➡ 224. **True.** The difference in gravity means a person could likely jump three times higher on Mars than on Earth.

⇛ 225. **False.** It takes almost twice as long (687 days) for Mars to rotate around the sun as it takes Earth (365¼ days).

⇨ 226. **False.** Snow is translucent, not white. But due to the way those clear translucent crystals reflect light, it appears white to the human eye.

227. SNOWFLAKES GET BIGGER AT COLDER TEMPERATURES.

TRUE OR FALSE?

228. MARS HAS BLUE SUNSETS.

TRUE OR FALSE?

229. THERE ARE THOUSANDS OF LIGHTNING FLASHES ON EARTH EVERY MINUTE.

TRUE OR FALSE?

230. THE SINGLE ICE AGE IN EARTH'S HISTORY TOOK PLACE ABOUT 8,000 YEARS AGO.

TRUE OR FALSE?

231. LIGHT AND SOUND BOTH TRAVEL AT THE SAME SPEED.

TRUE OR FALSE?

➠ 227. **False.** Snowflakes get smaller when the temperature drops.

➜ 228. **True.** The red planet has blue sunsets.

✏ 229. **True.** More than 8 million cloud-to-ground lighting strikes happen per day worldwide.

➠ 230. **False.** Scientists believe there have been at least five ice ages in Earth's history. The most recent, usually known as "the last glacial period," ended about 11,700 years ago.

➜ 231. **False.** Light travels at 186,000 miles per second (299,792,458 meters per second). At room temperature, sound travels at 767 miles per hour (1,235 km/h).

232. A POUND OF STEEL WEIGHS MORE THAN A POUND OF FEATHERS.

TRUE OR FALSE? ➡ ➡ ➡ ➡

233. IN A VACUUM, A POUND OF STEEL WILL FALL FASTER FROM A BUILDING THAN A POUND OF FEATHERS.

TRUE OR FALSE? ➤➤ ➤➤ ➤➤ ➤➤

234. THE SOUTH POLE CAN HAVE 24 HOURS OF SUNLIGHT.

TRUE OR FALSE? ⊃ ⊃ ⊃ ⊃

235. HURRICANES SPIN COUNTERCLOCKWISE THROUGHOUT THE WORLD.

TRUE OR FALSE? ➔ ➔ ➔ ➔

236. LIMESTONE IS MADE OF SEASHELLS.

TRUE OR FALSE? ➤ ➤ ➤ ➤

232. **False.** A pound of steel is denser than a pound of feathers but they both weigh the same.

233. **False.** When there is no friction, everything that weighs the same falls at the same rate.

234. **True.** In parts of Antarctica, the sun stays above the horizon line from late October until late February, giving each day 24 hours of sunlight.

235. **False.** South of the Equator, hurricanes spin clockwise.

236. **True.** Limestone is made of seashells and the bodies of tiny sea creatures.

237. QUARTZ NATURALLY COMES IN MANY COLORS.

TRUE OR FALSE? ➡ ➡ ➡ ➡

238. HURRICANES AND TORNADOS ARE THE SAME THING.

TRUE OR FALSE? ⇒ ⇒ ⇒ ⇒

239. NASA APOLLO MISSIONS 11, 12, 13, 14, 15, 16, AND 17 ALL LANDED ON THE MOON.

TRUE OR FALSE? ⇨ ⇨ ⇨ ⇨

240. MICROSOFT AND APPLE WERE STARTED IN GARAGES.

TRUE OR FALSE? ⇢ ⇢ ⇢ ⇢

241. THERE'S A WORD TO DESCRIBE THE FEAR OF BEING WITHOUT A CELLPHONE.

TRUE OR FALSE? → → → →

→ *237.* **True.** Quartz can be purple, brown, yellow, pink, or a mix of colors.

⟹ *238.* **False.** Hurricanes form over water. Tornados form over land.

⇨ *239.* **False.** NASA's *Apollo 13* was supposed to land on the moon, but an explosion forced it to return to Earth without landing on the moon's surface.

⇢ *240.* **True.** Tech giants Microsoft, Apple, Google, and HP all launched in garages before the companies had office space.

→ *241.* **True.** Nomophobia is the fear of being without a cellphone.

242. ASIDE FROM THE SUN, THE BRIGHTEST STAR IN EARTH'S SKY IS POLARIS, THE NORTH STAR.

TRUE OR FALSE?

243. MORE PEOPLE IN THE WORLD HAVE MOBILE PHONES THAN INDOOR TOILETS.

TRUE OR FALSE?

MOBILE PHONES THAN INDOOR

TRUE OR FALSE?

242. **False.** The brightest star as viewed from Earth is Sirius, the Dog Star.

243. **True.** Mobile phones are far more common than indoor plumbing in some parts of the world.

Sports

244. THERE ARE FOUR BASES IN BASEBALL.

TRUE OR FALSE?   →   →   →   →

245. LACROSSE IS A NATIONAL SPORT OF CANADA.

TRUE OR FALSE?   ➡   ➡   ➡   ➡

246. ARGENTINA HAS PLAYED IN EVERY FIFA WORLD CUP MEN'S SOCCER TOURNAMENT.

TRUE OR FALSE?   ⟫→   ⟫→   ⟫→   ⟫→

→ 244. **True.** There are first, second, third, and home bases in baseball.

➡ 245. **True.** While ice hockey is the national winter sport of Canada, lacrosse is the national summer sport.

➡➡ 246. **False.** Brazil is only team to have played in every World Cup men's soccer tournament.

247. "FOX TOSSING" WAS ONCE A POPULAR SPORT.

TRUE OR FALSE? ⊃ ⊃ ⊃ ⊃

248. THE OLYMPICS USED TO AWARD MEDALS FOR ART.

TRUE OR FALSE? → → → →

See the back of the page to find out.

247. **True.** Fox tossing was popular among Europe's aristocracy in the 17th and 18th centuries.

248. **True.** From 1912 to 1948, the Olympics awarded medals to "sports-inspired" fine arts, in categories such as painting, sculpture, architecture, literature, and music.

249. There are six rings in the Olympic symbol.

TRUE OR FALSE? ➤ ➤ ➤ ➤

250. All golf balls have 442 dimples.

TRUE OR FALSE? → → → →

251. Barry Bonds holds the record for the most home runs in a season.

TRUE OR FALSE? ⇨ ⇨ ⇨ ⇨

252. There are three sports in a triathlon.

TRUE OR FALSE? ⇒ ⇒ ⇒ ⇒

253. The first nation after Greece to host the Olympic Games was France.

TRUE OR FALSE? → → → →

➤ *249.* **False.** There are five rings in the Olympic symbol.

➡ *250.* **False.** There is no standard number of dimples on a golf ball, but most have between 300 and 450.

⇨ *251.* **True.** Barry Bonds hit 73 home runs playing for the San Francisco Giants in 2001.

⇢ *252.* **True.** Bicycling, running, and swimming are the three sports in a triathlon.

➡ *253.* **True.** The modern Olympic Games were revived in Greece, in 1896, and then hosted in 1900 in Paris, France.

254. THE ONLY FOOTBALL TEAM TO HAVE A PERFECT SEASON IS THE GREEN BAY PACKERS.

TRUE OR FALSE?

255. IN AMERICAN FOOTBALL, A FIELD GOAL IS 2 POINTS.

TRUE OR FALSE?

256. BASEBALL IS THE MOST POPULAR SPECTATOR SPORT IN THE UNITED STATES.

TRUE OR FALSE?

257. BASKETBALL WAS FIRST PLAYED IN SPRINGFIELD, MASSACHUSETTS.

TRUE OR FALSE?

✏️ 254. **False.** The 1972 Miami Dolphins are the only team ever to have a perfect season. The Dolphins had an undefeated regular season and then won three postseason games, including the Super Bowl.

➤➤ 255. **False.** A field goal is 3 points in American football.

➤ 256. **False.** Football is the most popular spectator sport in the United States. About 37 percent of Americans say it is their favorite sport.

➤ 257. **True.** Basketball began in 1891 in Springfield, Massachusetts.

258. FIRST-PLACE WINNERS IN THE OLYMPICS HAVE ALWAYS RECEIVED GOLD MEDALS.

TRUE OR FALSE?

259. A MARATHON IS 50 KILOMETERS LONG.

TRUE OR FALSE?

See the back of the page to find out. 145

➳ 258. **False.** In Ancient Greece, winners received olive wreaths. At the first modern Olympics in 1896, first place winners won silver medals and their runners-up received copper medals.

◯ 259. **False.** A marathon is 26.2 miles (42.2 km) long.

260. SERENA WILLIAMS HAS WON MORE GRAND SLAM SINGLES TENNIS TOURNAMENTS THAN HER OLDER SISTER, VENUS WILLIAMS.

TRUE OR FALSE? ➔ ➔ ➔ ➔

261. TUG-OF-WAR USED TO BE AN OLYMPIC SPORT.

TRUE OR FALSE? ➢ ➢ ➢ ➢

262. TIGER WOODS WAS 18 YEARS OLD WHEN HE WON HIS FIRST MASTERS GOLF TOURNAMENT.

TRUE OR FALSE? ➔ ➔ ➔ ➔

263. NBA STANDS FOR NATIONAL BOWLING ASSOCIATION.

TRUE OR FALSE? ⇒ ⇒ ⇒ ⇒

→ *260.* **True.** Serena Williams has won more than three times as many Grand Slam singles tennis titles as Venus Williams.

➤ *261.* **True.** Between 1900 and 1920, tug-of-war was an Olympic team sport.

➡ *262.* **False.** Tiger Woods was 21 when he won his first Masters golf tournament in 1997.

⇒ *263.* **False.** NBA stands for National Basketball Association.

264. In soccer, the player cannot touch the ball with his or her head.

TRUE OR FALSE? ⇨ ⇨ ⇨ ⇨

265. College football rules once outlawed the forward pass.

TRUE OR FALSE? ⇨ ⇨ ⇨ ⇨

266. There are 108 double stitches on a regulation baseball.

TRUE OR FALSE? → → → →

267. Professional soccer games are 60 minutes long.

TRUE OR FALSE? ✏ ✏ ✏ ✏

Answers for previous page.

> 264. **False.** Heading the ball is permitted in soccer, but players cannot touch the ball with their hands (except for the goalie).

> 265. **True.** The rules were changed in 1906 to make the forward pass a legal play in football.

> 266. **True.** Each baseball always has 108 double stitches. In Major League Baseball games, balls are only used for an average of six pitches before being replaced.

> 267. **False.** Soccer games are 90 minutes long, with referees allowed to add more minutes to the end of each half as they see fit.

THE WORLD ALMANAC™
AWESOME
TRUE-or-FALSE
QUESTIONS
FOR
SMART KIDS
-ANIMALS-

COMING SOON